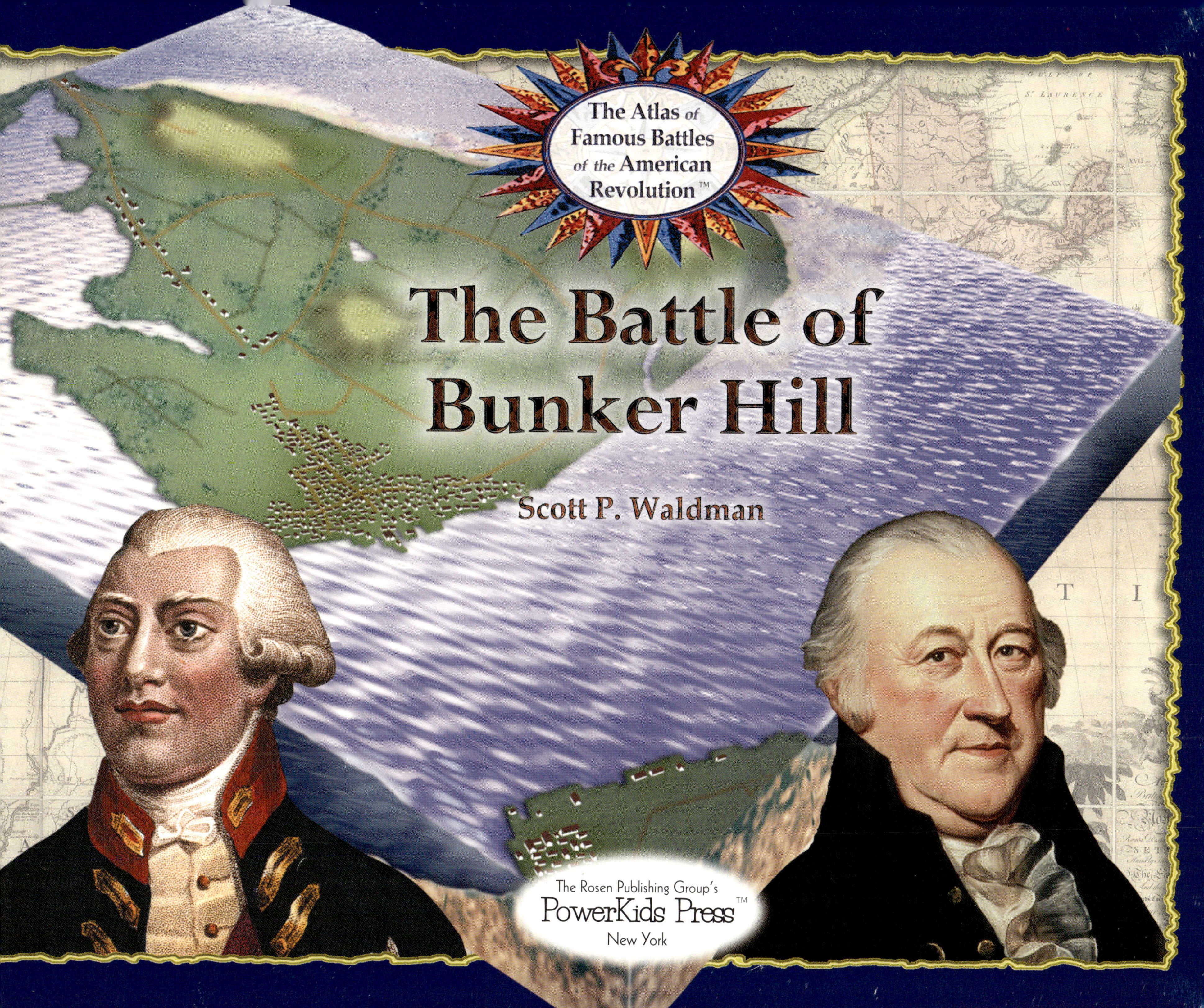
The Atlas of
Famous Battles
of the American
Revolution™
The Battle of
Bunker Hill
Scott P. Waldman
The Rosen Publishing Group's
PowerKids Press™
New York

Published in 2003 by The Rosen Publishing Group, Inc.
29 East 21st Street, New York, NY 10010

First Edition

Editor: Nancy MacDonell Smith

Book Design: Michael J. Caroleo

Photo Credits: Cover, title page, pp. 15, 16 (3-D map) by Maria E. Melendez; cover, title page, p. 4 (King George III), p. 11 (inset) © Bettmann/CORBIS; cover, title page, p. 7 (Ward) © Independence National Historical Park; pp. 4 (illustration), 7 (lower right), 8, 11 (map), 12 (illustration), 15 (illustration bottom and inset left), 15 (firing from redoubt), 16 (illustration bottom), 19 (illustration), 20 (inset) © North Wind Pictures; pp. 4 (map), 7 (map), 20 (map) by Michael Jacobsen; pp. 8 (bottom) Emmett Collection; p. 16 (inset) © Print Collection Miriam and Ira D. Wallach Division of Art, Prints and Photographs, The New York Public Library Astor, Lennox and Tilden Foundations; p. 11 (bottom right) courtesy, U.S. Navy Historical Center; pp. 12 (plate, knife and fork), 15 (rifle), 16 (sword and bayonet), 19 (rifle) © George C. Neumann Collection, Valley Forge National Historic Park, photos by Cindy Reiman; pp. 12 (map), 19 (map) © Library of Congress; p. 20 (illustration bottom) National Gallery of Art, Washington, gift of Edgar William and Bernice Chrysler Garbisch.

Waldman, Scott P.
The Battle of Bunker Hill / by Scott P. Waldman.
p. cm. — (The atlas of famous battles of the American Revolution)
Includes bibliographical references and index.
ISBN 0-8239-6329-2 (lib. bdg.)
1. Bunker Hill, Battle of, 1775—Juvenile literature. [1. Bunker Hill, Battle of, 1775. 2. United States—History—Revolution, 1775–1783—Campaigns.] I. Title. II. Series.
E241.B9 W17 2003
973.3'312—dc21

2001007776

Manufactured in the United States of America

Contents

George III was 37 years old and had been king for 15 years when the American Revolution started.

At the time that Governor Gage declared martial law, the population of Boston was about 16,000. It was the third largest town in North America.

After Lexington and Concord

On June 12, 1775, about two months after the Battle of Lexington and Concord, General Thomas Gage, the governor of Massachusetts, declared **martial law**. Shops and businesses in Boston were closed. The only sound heard in the streets was that of soldiers marching. British soldiers, who were known as **regulars**, had about 5,000 troops. The colonists numbered 10,000 men. Regulars had placed **barricades** around the city and near government buildings. During this time, the colonists had gathered around the city. The British realized that they could be attacked at any time. To prevent this, they would have to capture Dorchester Heights and Charlestown **Peninsula**, which were across Boston Harbor from the city of Boston. There were high hills in this area that could be used to defend or to attack the city. King George III sent three generals to help beat the colonists. The generals were planning to break through the line of colonists around Boston. The colonists learned of this plan and came up with one of their own.

Dorchester Heights and Charlestown Peninsula were important. They lay on either side of Boston Harbor and could be used to attack or to defend the city. Both sides wanted to control these peninsulas.

Planning for a Battle

On June 16, 1775, the colonists made the first move. The commander of the American **militia** in Boston was a man named Artemis Ward, a former politician. Ward decided that the militia would have to act quickly if they were to stop a British attack. Colonist spies discovered that the British were planning to attack within the next few days. Colonel William Prescott, a farmer and a war veteran, gathered a force of about 1,000 men on Cambridge Common, across the Charles River from Boston. Prescott's plan was to **fortify** Bunker Hill before dawn. Bunker Hill was the tallest hill on the Charlestown Peninsula. None of the men in the militia wore uniforms. Many of them had just come from work. They carried their **ammunition** in bags around their necks. The men waited until about 9:00 P.M. to start marching. They would have to work all night to surprise the British by dawn. The colonists had **pickaxes** and shovels with them. These tools were an important part of their plan.

American troops, pulling several wagons full of tools, marched north from Cambridge to the Charlestown Peninsula, where they got ready for battle with the British. **Bottom:** *The militia were not professional soldiers. They were ordinary citizens who left their jobs to fight in the American Revolution.*

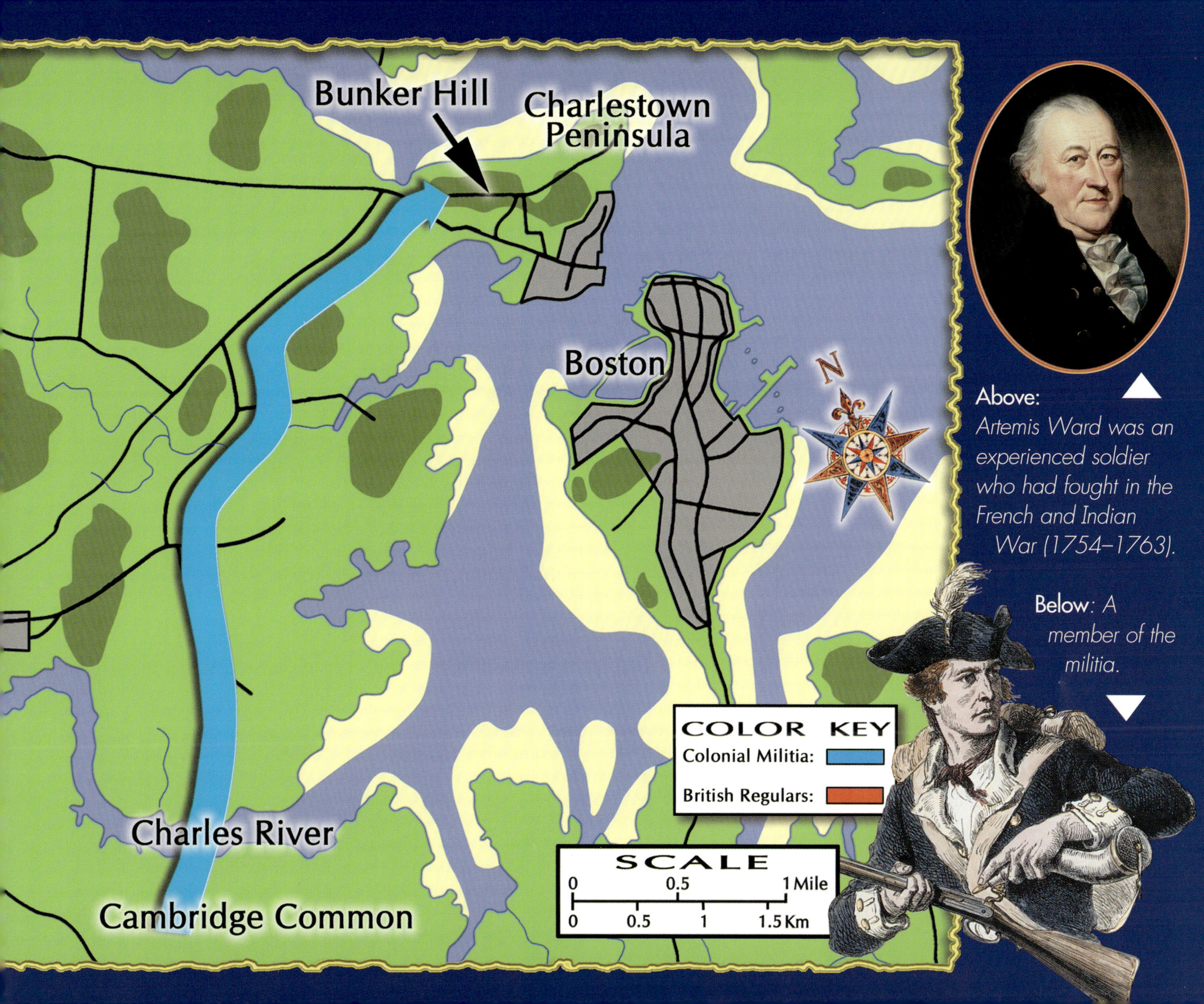

Above: *Artemis Ward was an experienced soldier who had fought in the French and Indian War (1754–1763).*

Below: *A member of the militia.*

Bunker Hill and Breed's Hill are about half a mile (1 km) apart.

This engraving shows how the redoubt on the top of Breed's Hill looked. The militia had just a few hours to build this large structure.

A Change in Plans

When he reached Bunker Hill, Colonel Prescott changed his original plan. Instead of fortifying Bunker Hill, he would fortify the smaller Breed's Hill. Despite this change, the battle would become known as the Battle of Bunker Hill. At about midnight, the men began their difficult work. They were building a mound of earth, known as a **redoubt**, used for cover from enemy fire on the top of Breed's Hill. The redoubt would be 160 feet (49 m) long and 80 feet (24 m) wide. It was going to have a 6-foot-tall (2-m-tall) wall made of earth protecting it. The men worked quickly and quietly. They dug a floor and used the shoveled dirt to build the walls. The men put branches, mud, and barrels in the wall to make it more solid. The men built a **breastwork**, which was a few feet (m) high from the redoubt to the base of the hill. As the sun rose, the men were tired from working hard.

Right: *The men building the redoubt worked for hours without food or water.*

The Battle Begins

At dawn on June 17, sailors on the British ship *Lively* saw the redoubt and began firing cannons at it. The ship was too far away to do much damage. However, it was close enough to shock many of the colonists, who had never experienced battle. A cannon **shell** hit one of the important water tanks in the redoubt. Another shell hit a man working outside the redoubt. The men started to realize the danger they faced. They had been working all night, and they still had no food or water. Many snuck away before the real fighting began. General Ward did not send many men to Breed's Hill. He wanted to keep most of his troops closer to Boston, where they could defend the colonists who had gathered around the city. Meanwhile, British general Gage watched the action on Breed's Hill from a nearby location. He prepared himself for battle.

Lively *was too far away to do much damage to the redoubt, but one member of the militia was killed by its cannon fire.* **Top:** *General Thomas Gage had been commander in chief of the British forces in North America since 1763. He became governor of Massachusetts in 1775.* **Bottom:** Lively *was a large warship, one of several British crafts that were in Boston Harbor at the time.*

Bunker Hill
Breed's Hill
Redoubt
COLOR KEY
Colonial Militia:
British Regulars:
SCALE (Yards)
50
200
400
600
0
100
300
500
Lively

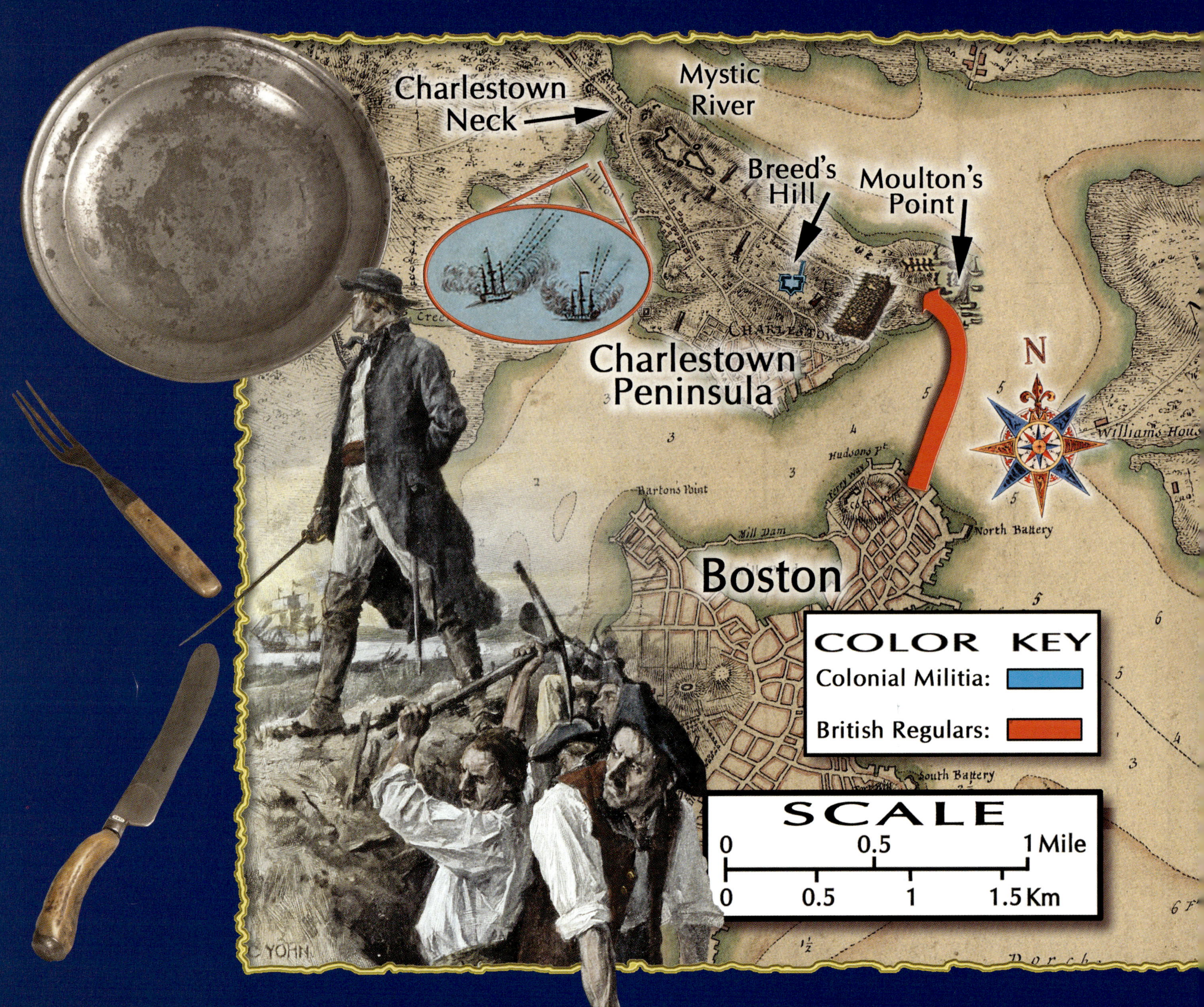
Charlestown Neck
Mystic River
Breed's Hill
Moulton's Point
Charlestown Peninsula
N
Boston
Barton's Point
Mill Dam
North Battery
South Battery
Hudsons Pt
Williams House
COLOR KEY
Colonial Militia:
British Regulars:
SCALE
0
0.5
1 Mile
0
0.5
1
1.5 Km

The British Land

Colonel Prescott noticed that his tired troops were ready to give up. He jumped up on the breastwork wall and walked up and down its length, joking with the men. The colonel's actions gave the men courage, and they began to work faster. The colonists also fortified an old fence and a stone wall. Behind them the Mystic River provided a natural boundary. This prevented the British from surrounding the hill. General Gage and his officers decided that a **head-on** attack of the redoubt would be the best **strategy**. The regulars began landing at Moulton's Point on the tip of the Charlestown Peninsula at about 1:00 P.M. They gathered at the base of Breed's Hill, where they sat down and ate lunch. The colonists watched nervously. They still had no food. The British kept Charlestown Neck, the area connecting the peninsula to the mainland, under constant fire so that American **reinforcements** would have trouble getting to Breed's Hill.

From Moulton's Point, the British marched inland to Breed's Hill, where the colonists were waiting. **Inset:** *Colonel Prescott's walk along the top of the redoubt to encourage the men was a bold move for a senior officer. Normally officers did not walk where they could easily be shot.* **Far Left:** *The regulars used plates and utensils like these, from the 1770s, when they sat down to eat lunch.*

The First Attack

The British set up cannons on Copp's Hill in Boston and fired at the colonists. At about 2:00 P.M., one group of British soldiers advanced on the men hiding behind the fence. Another group of regulars moved toward the breastwork. They had trouble walking uphill because of their heavy packs. The colonists let the British get very close before firing, so that there would be a better chance of hitting the **targets**. The colonists were instructed to shoot at the officers, because officers gave the orders on the battlefield. Without their officers, the regulars wouldn't know what to do. Most of the colonists' shots hit their targets, and many regulars were either killed or wounded. The British gathered at the bottom of the hill and began another attack. The second attack was deadlier for the British than was the first one. The Americans felt that they might win the battle. However, they were running out of ammunition.

The militia fired at the British from the top of Breed's Hill, in the middle of the Charlestown Peninsula. **Inset Left:** *The colonists waited until they could see the whites of the British soldiers' eyes before they fired.* **Inset Right:** *The packs carried by British soldiers weighed more than 50 lbs (23 kg).* **Top:** *This is one of the many different kinds of rifles used by the colonists.*

Bunker Hill
Breed's Hill
Charlestown Peninsula
N
COLOR KEY
Colonial Militia:
British Regulars:

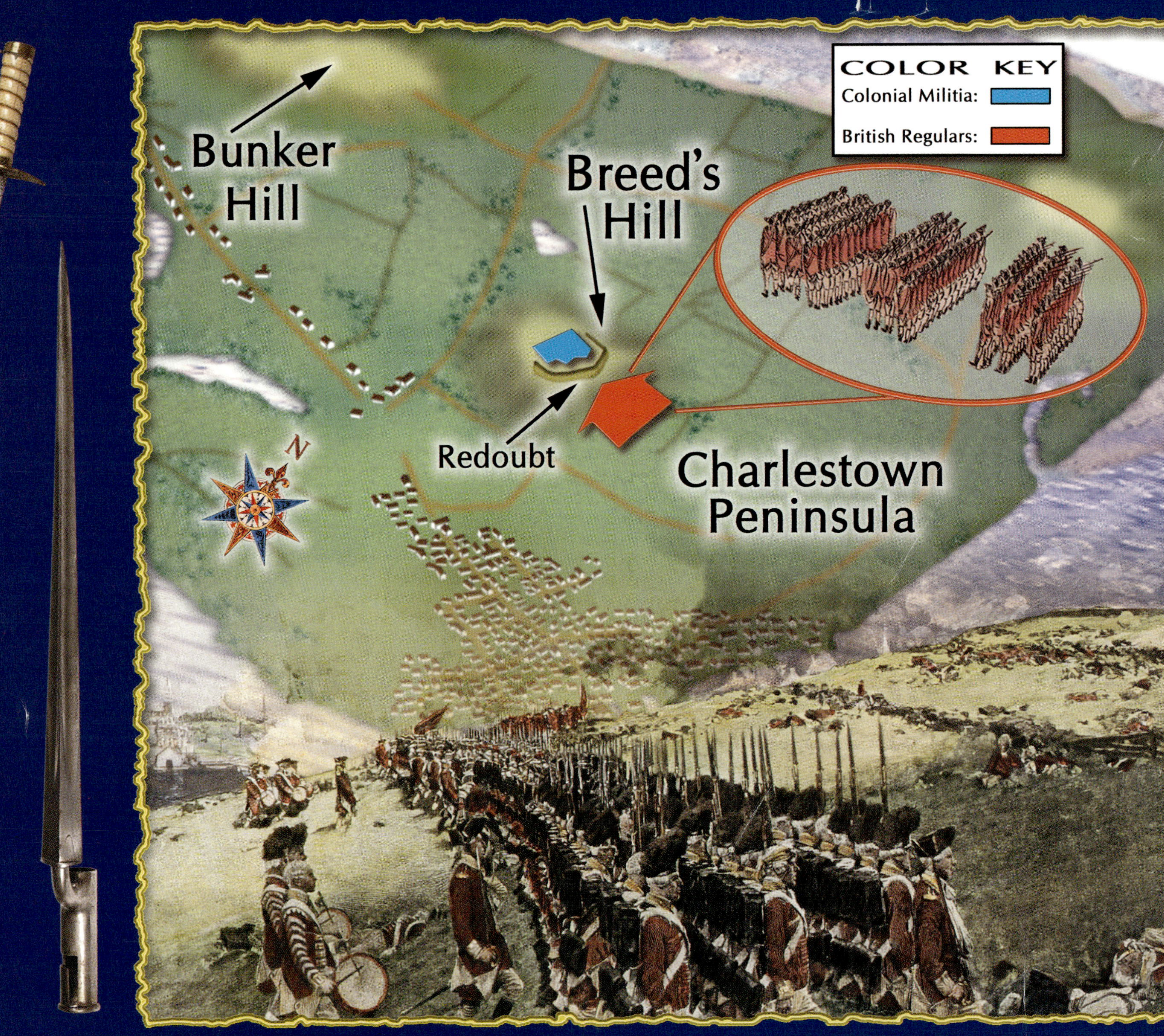
COLOR KEY
Colonial Militia:
British Regulars:
Bunker Hill
Breed's Hill
Redoubt
N
Charlestown Peninsula

The Final Charge

At about 4:30 P.M., the regulars made their final charge. They **stormed** the breastwork. Several regulars were killed in the attack. The colonists behind the breastwork could no longer hold off the British. Many of the colonists ran to the redoubt. The regulars then attacked the redoubt. The general in charge of the regulars had allowed them to take off their heavy packs. This let them move more easily. The colonists fired their last rounds at the advancing regulars. Many regulars were killed. However, it only slowed down the British troops instead of stopping them. The colonists quickly ran out of ammunition. The regulars climbed the walls of the redoubt and used their **bayonets** to attack the colonists. The colonists fought back with swords and the ends of their **muskets**. It was the deadliest fighting of the day for both sides. In the end, the Americans were **overpowered** by the British.

The colonists retreated to the redoubt after the British took over the breastwork. **Far Left:** *The colonists used swords like this one to try to force the British back from the redoubt.* **Left:** *The bayonets used by the regulars were about 21 inches (53 cm) long.* **Inset:** *The regulars marched up Breed's Hill in formation, as they were trained to do.*

The Colonists Turn Back

Prescott realized that his men would be killed if they stayed in the redoubt. He ordered his men to **retreat**. The colonists gathered at Bunker Hill as the British took control of the abandoned redoubt on Breed's Hill. The regulars then continued on to Bunker Hill. The colonists decided to run away, because they didn't want to be killed by the advancing regulars. The retreating colonists still had to pass through Charlestown Neck to get away from the British and back to the mainland. This area was dangerous because it was being shot at by two British ships. These ships were also firing at Charlestown. This set a number of the town's buildings on fire. By 5:00 P.M., the British had taken control of both Bunker Hill and Breed's Hill.

To retreat from the advancing British troops, the colonists had to get across Charlestown Neck, a very narrow strip of land. **Inset:** *At the fiercest point in the battle, the British soldiers and the colonists fought hand to hand. Many men on both sides were killed that day.* **Far Right:** *This rifle, known as a Brown Bess, was used by the regulars during the American Revolution.*

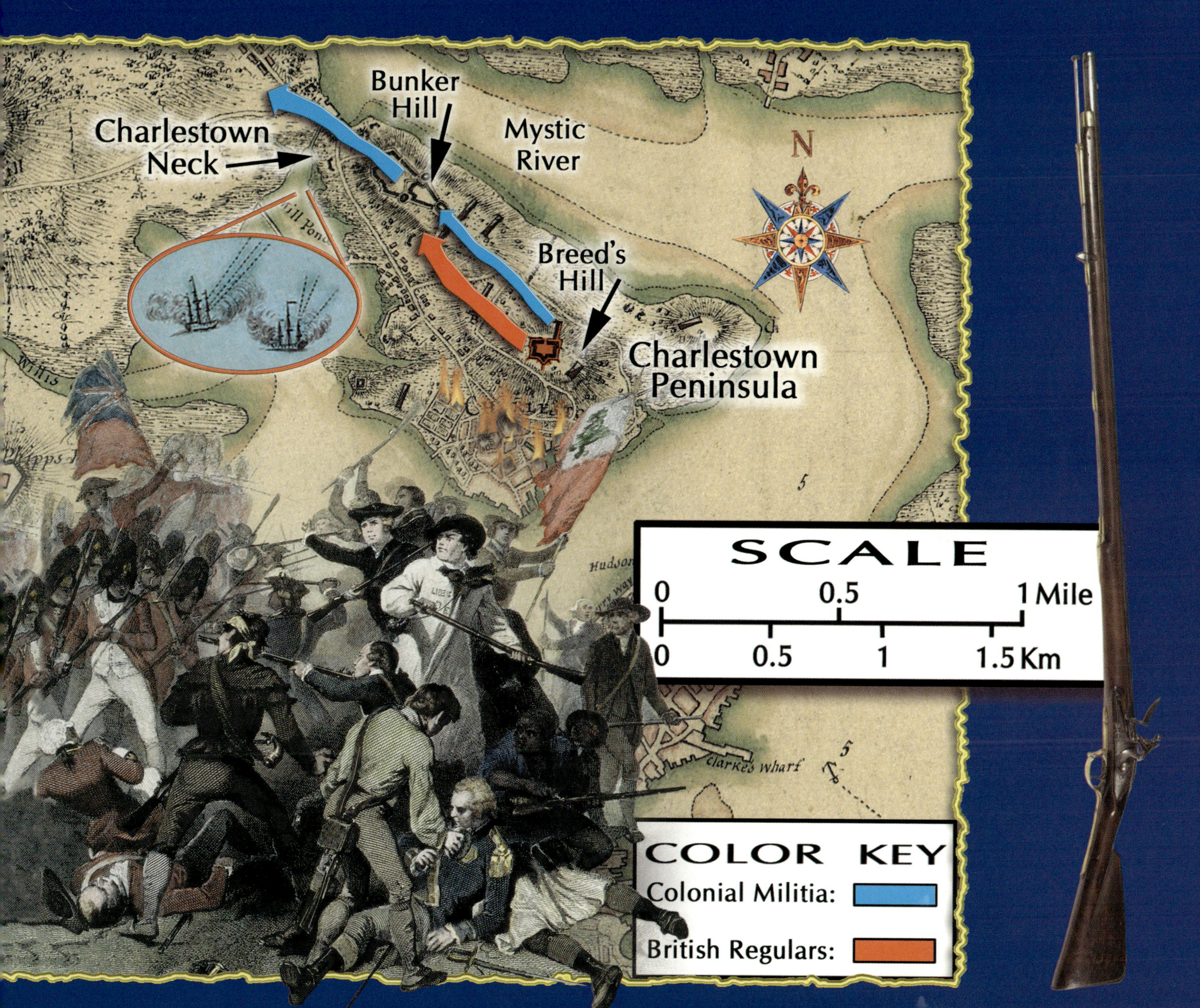
Bunker Hill
Charlestown Neck
Mystic River
N
Breed's Hill
Charlestown Peninsula
SCALE
0
0.5
1 Mile
0
0.5
1
1.5 Km
COLOR KEY
Colonial Militia:
British Regulars:

Charlestown
Peninsula
SCALE
0
0.5
1 Mile
0
0.5
1
1.5 Km
N
Boston
CHARLES TOWN
BOSTON

The Results

Everyone in the area, both British and American, was very concerned about the outcome of the battle. Many of them had loved ones on the battlefield. Breed's Hill was on a raised peninsula that faced Boston. This meant that people around Boston Harbor could see the fighting. The thick, black smoke from the **gunpowder** could be seen many miles (km) away. In the towns surrounding Boston, people went to the nearest high point to see what was happening on Breed's Hill. Many Americans saw their troops drive back two British charges. The British suffered more than 1,100 **casualties** in the fighting that day. The Americans had between 400 and 600 casualties. Most of the American casualties happened during the retreat. Hundreds of colonists had stopped fighting and had gone home before the battle ended. The colonists lost the battle, but they proved that they could stand up to the regulars.

The fighting on the Charlestown Peninsula was visible for miles (km) around. **Top:** *Colonists in the surrounding towns climbed up to their roofs and other high points to watch the battle.* **Bottom:** *Cannons firing from British ships set fire to houses in Charlestown.*

A Country United

The Battle of Lexington and Concord proved that the Americans were willing to fight for fair treatment. The Battle of Bunker Hill proved that they could organize an army. The colonists at Breed's Hill had fought bravely without food, water, or reinforcements. More colonists began to doubt the leadership of the British.

On July 3, 1775, General George Washington took over the command of the troops surrounding Boston. By March 1776, Washington had driven the British out of Boston for good. It had taken him only eight months. There were no more major battles in Boston. General Washington lost only 20 soldiers during this time. Gage was removed from his post as governor of Massachusetts. The British government felt that he should have been able to beat the colonists. The American colonists had taken another major step toward independence from their British rulers.

Glossary

ammunition (am-yoo-NIH-shun) The materials used for attacking or defending a position, such as the bullets or other items fired from guns.
barricades (BA-rih-kaydz) Things that block something else from passing.
bayonets (bay-oh-NETS) Knives attached to the front ends of rifles.
breastwork (BREST-werk) A wall built for protection.
casualties (KA-zhul-teez) People who have been injured or killed in battle.
fortify (FOR-tih-fy) To make strong.
gunpowder (GUN-pow-dur) A black powder that explodes in a gun and moves the bullet.
head-on (HED-ON) To meet someone or something directly.
martial law (MAR-shul LAW) The law applied by the military in an occupied territory.
militia (muh-LIH-shuh) A group of people who are trained and ready to fight in an emergency.
muskets (MUS-kits) Guns with long barrels used in battle and hunting.
overpowered (oh-ver-POW-urd) To have been much stronger or greater than something.
peninsula (puh-NIN-suh-luh) An area of land surrounded by water on three sides.
pickaxes (pik-aks-ez) Tools with one sharp end and one flat end, used for digging.
redoubt (rih-DOWT) A small fort with walls made of earth.
regulars (REH-gyuh-lerz) British soldiers.
reinforcements (ree-in-FORS-mentz) Fresh soldiers sent to help an army.
retreat (ree-TREET) To back away from a fight.
shell (SHEL) Something fired out of a rifle or cannon.
stormed (STORMD) Attacked.
strategy (STRA-tuh-jee) The science of planning and directing large-scale military operations.
targets (TAR-gits) Things that are aimed at.

Index

Primary Sources

Cover, Page 7. *Artemis Ward.* Oil on canvas, Charles Willson Peale, 1794–95. Independence National Park collection. Peale was one of the most important American artists of his time. As a young man he studied in London with the artist Benjamin West. West, an American-born painter, was a favorite of King George III. After his studies Peale returned to the colonies, where he painted portraits of many famous Americans, including George Washington, Martha Washington, Thomas Jefferson, and Alexander Hamilton. **Page 12. (Left).** *Soldier's plate, knife, and fork.* Pewter, steel, and bone, c. 1750–99. The George C. Neumann Collection at Valley Forge National Historic Park. At the time of the American Revolution, most people carried knives and forks with them when they traveled because inns and restaurants did not always provide guests with eating utensils. Pewter, steel, and bone were common materials. **(Inset).** *Colonel Prescott Walking Along the Redoubt.* Print, artist, and date unknown. Emmett Collection, Miriam and Ira D. Wallach Division of Arts, Prints, and Photographs, The New York Public Library, Astor, Lenox, and Tilden Foundations. Thomas Abbis Emmett was a doctor in late nineteenth-century America. He collected early American prints, which he donated to the New York Public Library. This print shows Colonel Prescott's heroism and dedication to the cause of American independence. By putting himself in the line of fire, Prescott was doing something very unusual for an officer at the time of the American Revolution. Officers usually stayed where they were less likely to get killed. **Page 15.** *Attack on Bunker's Hill, With the Burning of Charles Town.* Oil on canvas, artist unknown, c. 1783. National Gallery of Art. This painting, one of the most commonly reproduced images of the American Revolution, was given to the National Gallery by Edgar William and Bernice Chrysler Garbisch in 1953. Though the painting dates from the time of the American Revolution, it wasn't widely reproduced until the hundredth anniversary of the revolution. Americans at that time were very interested in how their country became independent. Many newspapers ran special prints of this and other paintings of battles of the American Revolution. Americans put up these prints on their walls to show how proud they were of their country. **Page 16 (Left).** *Sword and Bayonet.* Steel, c. 1770s. The George C. Neumann Collection at Valley Forge National Historic Park. During the eighteenth century, swords were carried by officers as a sign of their high rank. Bayonets were used by ordinary professional soldiers. The colonists had to be trained by European officers in the use of bayonets, because most of them had not used this type of weapon before. **(Inset).** *British March Up Breed's Hill.* Color illustration, Howard Pyle, 1898. Delaware Museum of Art. Pyle was a popular children's book illustrator of the nineteenth century. He liked to draw exciting historical scenes that would make the past seem real to his readers. Pyle ran a free art school that was attended by many illustrators who went on to become very successful, including N. C. Wyeth.

Web Sites

Due to the changing nature of Internet links, PowerKids Press has developed an online list of Web sites related to the subject of this book. This site is updated regularly. Please use this link to access the list:

www.powerkidslinks.com/afbar/bunker/